THE STUDENT ATHLETE HANDBOOK FOR THE 21ST CENTURY

A GUIDE TO RECRUITING, SCHOLARSHIPS, AND PREPPING FOR COLLEGE

BY
CHRISTINE GRIMES

Copyright © 2006 by Christine Grimes
Images copyright © BigStockPhoto

First edition

Printed in the United States of America.

ISBN 978-1-4303-0901-7

TABLE OF CONTENTS

FOREWORD

Maybe you've always dreamed of playing ball for a Big 12 School, or maybe all you're looking for is a way to play for a couple more years and help pay your way through school. No matter what type of student athlete you are, this is the book for you! It will help you understand what it takes to become a collegiate athlete and what it takes to earn athletic scholarships. You'll learn about test-taking procedures, making the grades, how to make sure scouts see you, and how to secure your eligibility for athletic scholarships. You will also hear from coaches and professors on what they're looking for in a student athlete.

INTRODUCTION

I played competitive softball at a very young age, yet I found myself, a high school senior, sitting the bench for my team. Even though I had ten years of experience as a catcher, the new coach decided to make it a "building year," and I watched a sophomore take my place on varsity. But I went on to earn a Division II fastpitch scholarship, started as a freshman, and played in regional playoffs during my collegiate career.

How did all this happen? I learned the recruiting game. I highlighted my skills and marketed myself. I paid attention to my grades. I fixed my attitude. And I loved the game. By following the advice in this book, I discovered the world of college athletics.

When I began coaching, I discovered that there weren't any books for **today's** student athlete.

Yes, there were guides and resources, but they were plain—boring. They offered few pages of guidance but hundreds of pages of often outdated addresses and phone numbers that today's student could quickly find on the internet.

Over the last five years as a college instructor, I've learned today's youth are on top of the latest technology, web resources, and information. What they lack is advice from people in the know. What they want are real-life experiences, knowledge, and a guide to where they can find the rest. <u>The Student Athlete Handbook for the 21st Century</u> will give you everything you need to navigate the college scholarship and recruiting process. Whether you're a high-school student, a parent, a coach, or a counselor, this book is what you've been searching for.

CHAPTER 1 – MASTERING THE FUNDAMENTALS

So how do you get an athletic scholarship? What do you do? When do you start?

You start by educating yourself about the recruiting process. By understanding what coaches and scouts are looking for, you can make yourself the most desirable candidate possible.

You may start as early as your freshman year in high school, but it's never too late to improve your chances. Your first goal as a prospective student athlete should be to complete the minimum requirements, which include taking core courses, maintaining a passing grade point average, earning a qualifying score on the SAT or ACT, and of course, graduating from high school.

Coaches look for potential players one to five years down the road. They may be looking to fill new slots on their teams, or they may be watching for upcoming players who could replace an athlete graduating in three years. Depending upon the level of play, coaches may do the recruiting themselves, or they may send out scouts and recruiters to find potential athletes.

Coaches are looking for players who will perform well and fit in with their team and school. When you are recruited, you're essentially taking on a job. The coach will pay for your schooling in return for your performance and participation on the team. As a student athlete, it is your **job** to play ball. It is your **job** to show up on time, practice, go to class, study, pass your classes, play, perform on the field or court, and represent the school and your team.

WIN

KEEP IMPORTANT DOCUMENTS ON FILE

Make a folder for your
Transcripts
Letters
Test scores (SAT, ACT)
College brochures
Team media guide
Current stats
Newspaper clips

Different teams work and function in different ways, but coaches want players who will work for them and work with the other players. Coaches recruit whole people. From the very first meeting, coaches are evaluating whether you will be a good fit for their schools and their teams.

They will evaluate your letters, email, films, phone conversations, practices, and games. They may watch you warm up or evaluate your reaction to a big win or a big loss. They may ask other players and parents about your personality, your work ethic, and your team spirit. They are always recruiting and evaluating! As a player, you must always put your best foot forward, in class and in the game.

Once coaches discover you, the recruiting process begins. It's largely focused on the end of the junior year leading into the senior year, but don't wait for coaches to contact you! You can initiate contact with a letter or an email as early as your sophomore year.

A journey of a thousand miles must begin with a single step.

- Chinese proverb

Most schools begin early admissions a year in advance and open admissions in early February to late April of your senior year.

Don't wait until the summer after your senior year to be picked up. By then all the money will be gone!

It's a good idea for you to know what schools you're interested in by your junior year, certainly by the beginning of your senior year. Then you have several options as you begin talking with coaches. Financial aid forms are often due shortly after January of your senior year. Once you have been recruited, filled out your paperwork, and signed your contract, you'll finally be able to live the dream and play ball on a college scholarship!

The following chapters will walk you through each of these steps.

Below is a timeline of high school recruitment and preparation.

Freshman and Sophomore Year of High School
- Sign up for core classes, study for good grades
- Begin to research colleges
- Play on elite teams and travel teams for exposure

Sophomore Year and Entering into Junior Year
- Continue to establish good grades and take core classes
- Select about thirty schools to research
- Narrow your list to twenty and contact admissions offices for further info
- Break this list into three tiers:
  - Dream schools – ideal schools and scholarship picks
  - Realistic, solid schools – where you're likely to be admitted and recruited
  - Safety schools – sure of admission, sure of athletic ability and recruitment
- Contact coaches at these schools, introduce yourself by letter
- Attend skill camps

Beginning of Junior Year

- Familiarize yourself with recruitment windows and dead periods when you cannot meet with coaches (see NCAA and NAIA websites for sport-specific dates.)
- Contact coaches and introduce yourself by letter
- Take the SAT and ACT at least twice
- Be alert. At any time coaches may contact you and watch you play
- Attend college exposure camps

End of Junior Year

- Be aware of your recruitment windows and dead periods when you (and your parents) are not allowed to have contact with coaches. (According to the NCAA, "contact" means a face to face meeting, more than hello. Dead periods restrict "contact" but during these times you may still speak on the phone or by letter.)
- Register with Clearinghouse, which governs NCAA recruitment (you will need transcripts and SAT and ACT scores to do this)
- Begin a dialogue with coaches and schools you are most interested in

Senior Year
- Observe your recruitment windows and dead periods when you cannot meet with coaches
- Attend college exposure camps
- Continue dialogue with coaches.
- Visit several schools you are interested in
- Apply for admission
- File a FAFSA to be eligible for financial aid and scholarships
- Sign during Early and Regular signing periods for your National Letter of Intent

Once you have signed with a school, it's your job to be ready to play ball!

LOSS
IGNORING OTHER TYPES OF AID
Pursue academic, social club, individual, technical, and federal scholarships, grants, and aid.

CHAPTER 2
CHOOSING YOUR TEAM

What should you expect from collegiate play? Depending on your school, the level of competition and commitment will vary. Your year will probably include off-season play and training varying from daily morning weight 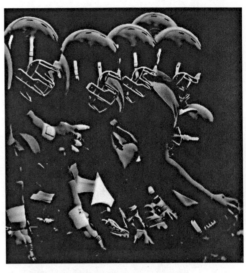 training and runs to travel and competition. During season, you may miss classes as many as two or three days a week. Registering for afternoon or Friday classes may be out of the question. Further, you'll need to have your work done when you return or be prepared for make-up tests or quizzes. All missed schoolwork will be your responsibility to make up, and you'll still need to make it to practices and additional training. Be prepared to spend early mornings and late nights training, practicing, and making up missed studies. It's likely your friends and social life will revolve around your teammates. But your level of play will determine how much time and effort you're expected to put in.

Only a small percentage of high school athletes go on to play at a collegiate level, and even fewer earn scholarships. Know that you must be talented, prepared, and hard-working to get what you want.

First, you must understand that there are different associations, divisions, and levels of play, which affect scholarships and aid.

Perhaps the most recognized is the National Collegiate Athletic Association, or NCAA, which has several divisions of play.

The National Association of Intercollegiate Athletics, or NAIA, has slightly simpler recruiting procedures.

You may also opt for the National Junior College Athletic Association, or NJCAA, which governs all two-year junior and community college athletics.

9

WIN
IMAGINE YOUR IDEAL COLLEGE, TEAM, AND PLAYING SEASON.
Think of how your expectations and ideals might fit into these categories.

Your association or division will impact the level of competition you'll experience as well as the amount of funding you'll receive.

By all means, apply to several different levels of play so you have options in your recruiting and collegiate application process.

LOSS
ASSUMING YOU'LL PLAY D-I.
There are many different levels of talent within Divisions. Don't limit your choices.

NCAA Division I

Division I is regarded as the premiere division of competition in collegiate sports. NCAA Division I Athletics follows more stringent recruiting regulations than other Divisions, and you'll be required to register with the Clearinghouse to declare your eligibility. These schools pick and choose from the best athletes in the nation and often have scholarships to fund most of their teams.

These scholarships may still range from partial to full-ride, but Division I schools have more funds, sponsors, and support to pass on to their teams. If you play for one of these teams, expect the best competition, the best equipment, and the best recognition. However, you should also expect the highest level of commitment and the least tolerance for student athletes failing to meet their expectations.

Most likely, athletics will be your priority at Division I schools. Everything else will have to work around your athletic schedule. You may be encouraged to take five years for your education, and you may find it difficult to take more than twelve hours a semester or to choose classes that are time-intensive. Plan to avoid courses that meet in the afternoon; they may conflict with practices.

These sacrifices may be worthwhile for some students and less so for others.

Find out more information about NCAA Divisions and sports teams at each school at the National Collegiate Athletic Association, www.NCAA.org

NCAA Division II

Division II Athletics offer a high level of competition with elite players, school funding, and scholarships. However, the competition, money, and recognition will be slightly less than Division I. These schools often recruit regionally rather than nationally and offer funding packages that pull from several resources. Division II's recruiting regulations are less stringent than Division I's, but you will still need to register with the Clearinghouse to declare your eligibility.

In Division II, you can afford to focus more on school. You'll have more freedom to choose courses and degree plans, and you may be able to graduate in four years. Also, you may be able to enroll in honors programs, which require more academic effort than mainstream classes. Athletics will still be a priority, but you may be treated as a student-athlete rather than an athlete-student. You'll still be required to perform in order to play, and you'll have to schedule classes and homework around practices, but this Division offers more freedom to students seeking some funding and competition.

NCAA Division III

Division III Athletics occupy the third and final tier of the NCAA. Division III offers students an opportunity to play ball at the collegiate level while focusing on their studies and their degree plans of choice. Competition in Division III is less intense than in Divisions I and II. These athletic programs often have very little funding, and these schools do not offer athletic scholarships. Coaches may work to find their students grants or scholarships from other sources, or may be able to find funds to support a small portion of tuition. Academics are expected to come first for players on these teams, but the athletic programs remain competitive and committed. To participate in this Division, you will have to declare your eligibility through the Clearinghouse.

To find NCAA rankings in all divisions, log on to NCAAsports.com

NAIA

The National Association of Intercollegiate Athletics is a separate division of collegiate athletics. Schools that belong to the NAIA participate in different recruiting procedures, athletic conferences, and competitions. NAIA schools offer the opportunity to play competitive collegiate athletics with some funding.

These schools focus on education while providing opportunities for competitive play. The intensity of competition varies depending upon school and region, but NAIA schools are commonly compared to schools in NCAA Divisions II or III.

The NAIA does not use the Clearinghouse to establish eligibility, so recruiting is more streamlined. For instance, NAIA coaches may approach players at any point, without waiting for dead periods or tournament play to end, and student athletes may leave one school and transfer to another without sitting out for a year. Funding at these schools is limited to school expenses like tuition and room and board.

Find out more information about NAIA teams at National Association of Intercollegiate Athletics, www.NAIA.org

NJCAA

The National Junior College Athletic Association is in charge of junior college and community college athletic programs.

Junior colleges (or community colleges) with athletic programs offer students a chance to gain more experience as both players and scholars before moving on to four-year schools. Junior colleges offer a lower-cost education while allowing students to play at a competitive level. Student athletes may choose to play for two years only or to pursue transfer scholarships from any four-year university. Many students choose junior colleges as stepping-stones in their college education. Also, many junior colleges offer athletic scholarships that partially or fully cover tuition. A junior college may offer the perfect opportunity for students who want to take college one step at a time.

Find out more information about NJCAA teams at National Junior College Athletic Association, www.NJCAA.org

These associations offer different levels of competition and funding and follow different recruiting procedures. Programs also vary greatly from school to school within these associations. Coaches and teams have very different approaches to discipline, performance, and academics. By looking at school websites and contacting coaches and admissions offices via email or letter, you can find out which schools and teams fit your needs.

Be practical when evaluating your athletic performance and choosing which associations and divisions to target. To judge your skill level, ask yourself the following questions.

> **WIN**
> **ATTEND A SKILLS CAMP**
> Participating in a sports camp will strengthen your fundamentals, teach you new skills and help you to evaluate your level of play. It will also give you the opportunity to interact with college players and coaches!

How many older players at your school have gone on to play in college? On scholarship? At what level? Are you the most talented athlete in your school? In your state?

Keep in mind that the most talented player in Rhode Island will be viewed differently than the most talented player in Texas. Be aware of your school's competition level. 5A-1A categories may change, but large schools and districts always have

tougher competition than smaller ones.
Participating on other teams and playing travel ball
may improve your chances.

Other factors will affect your marketability, too.
What position do you play? If a coach doesn't need
another shortstop or forward, can you play another
position? Are you willing to?
Also, teams usually have
more money reserved for
positions they need to fill,
such as quarterback or
pitcher. Attending camps
and learning new skills, will
increase your marketability.

Consider how much playing
time you want as well. You
may choose to play all the
time as a starter in a lower
division rather than playing
little for a more prestigious
Division I team.

**LOSS
CHOOSING A SCHOOL
OR A TEAM BECAUSE
SOMEONE ELSE WANTS
IT**
Choose your path based
on what you think will
be best for you. You
will be there for four
years of your life.
Trust your instincts.

Reflect on these issues and discuss them with your
parents, coaches, counselors, and peers.

**Do what you can, with what you
have, where you are.**
                                    -   **Theodore Roosevelt**

CHAPTER 3 ~
CRACKING THE BOOKS

So how do you know which schools to target and what to expect from them? Do your research! There's no excuse for not learning about schools you're interested in. If you don't know where to start, narrow your list of potential schools by determining what you want.

There are many questions to ask yourself before narrowing your search, including what you want from a school.

WIN
PICK A SCHOOL THAT FITS ALL OF YOUR NEEDS
To make the most of your college experience, find a school where you are comfortable with the campus, the team, the student body, and the location.

Are you looking for a large school with a lot of variety, large classes, diversity, and endless opportunities for student involvement, but little personal attention?

Or a small school with lots of personal attention, small classes and a community atmosphere, but with fewer choices for degrees and courses?

Also, where do you want to live? Do you prefer to stay close to home or try living in a new state for two to four years? Is there a school you'd want to attend even if you didn't participate in athletics?

What price range can you afford? You may say it depends on what kind of scholarship you can get. This is true, but you probably have an idea of where you sit among your peers. You may have scored a 1600 on the SAT or struggled through school. You may have the biggest house on the block or you may have held down an after-school job all through high school. Consider all of these factors. In the meantime, be aware of the costs of each school you're interested in. (That way, you'll know how much money *you or your parents* will pay out of pocket or borrow if you're unable to get financial aid.)

Do your research. Look online, take a trip to the local library, or head to the bookstore. Ask for help.

Find books that list top schools according to various criteria, including professions, degrees, location, price, value, safety, student life, etc. Then, decide which of these matter most and focus on schools that fit your new criteria. Often, price, location, and degree specialty will weigh heaviest in your decision-making.

Always bear in mind that your own resolution to success is more important than any other one thing.

- Abraham Lincoln

WHAT TO ASK YOURSELF WHEN CHOOSING POTENTIAL SCHOOLS

- What do I want to study?
- What type of classes and academic programs am I interested in?
- How long do I want to be in school?
- How much can I afford?
- How much aid do I need?
- Do I want to attend a public or a private school?
- Where do I want to live?
  - At home?
  - At school?
  - In state or out of state?
- Do I want to go to a big school or a little school?
- Am I interested in other activities besides sports?
- How do I evaluate myself as a player? As a person?
- Where will I thrive?
- What type of coach/coaching style am I looking for?
- What is important for me in a college?
  - Job placement?
  - Athletic reputation?
  - Degree plans?
  - Extracurricular experiences and opportunities?

When you first search for schools, be sure to include a couple that may not fit all of your criteria but catch your eye for some reason. You may find that these schools are a good fit, too, even if they aren't what you thought you wanted initially.

Don't rule out private schools simply because of cost or because they have a religious affiliation. Many private schools offer more scholarships to make up for higher tuition. Also, over half of the students at many "religious" universities are not affiliated with the school's sponsoring church.

Finally, choose a couple of "dream schools," a couple challenging schools, a few solid schools, and a few safe schools. Your first list may include thirty or forty schools and coaches if you start looking during or before your junior year.

It's a good idea to start with this many possibilities because it will help you to learn about a large number of schools and to determine what criteria you want to focus on.

> **LOSS**
> **PICKING A SCHOOL**
> **WITHOUT VISITING**
> Brochures and websites can only take you so far. Take a campus tour, drive around the neighborhoods, and find out where the stores are.

Don't narrow your selection to just one or two because coaches at those schools may not need or want you to play for them in your graduating year. When it comes time to speak with coaches, you'll narrow your focus further; for now, keep your options open.

Contact the schools. Once you have a list of schools you're interested in, get contact numbers, addresses, and email addresses for each school's admissions office, athletic office, *and* financial aid office. **Don't contact the coach yet.** You'll need to research the school and program first to make sure you're interested. It will also make you look more responsible if you know a little about a school before speaking to a coach. The best way to contact the school is via mail or email. **Get a professional sounding email address, not a novelty one with an obscure name.** Sign up for a new one at Yahoo!, Hotmail, or Gmail if necessary, and try to register for something simple that includes your name. Then make sure to check that address often. In your letter or message, include your contact information such as your name, address, phone number, and if applicable, email address. Address the school "To Whom It May Concern", state that you are interested in attending, include a little information about your high school or activities, and ask for information about the college.

Ask specifically for an admissions packet, a catalog, information on any degree programs or extracurricular activities you're interested in, and financial aid information. If there is a separate address for the financial aid office, contact this office and ask for all the information they give to prospective students. Also, if you are interested in a specialized degree program that's very competitive, a varsity sport, or any other specialized club—such as debate, student government, or campus ministry—ask for contact information for those groups and send those offices a letter asking for more information.

Try these websites for information on and rankings of universities and colleges

- For US News Annual College Rankings:
  Usnews.com/usnews/edu/
- For information on colleges and scholarships:
  Colleges.com
- For information about applying for college:
  Collegeanswer.com
- For information on the cost of schools:
  Princetonreview.com/college/
- To receive information on scholarships and find resources on admissions and financial aid, and to view freshman blogs:
  www.colleges.com

LOSS
SENDING SLOPPY MAIL
Rushing your work, sending sloppy emails, or failing to proofread will make you look lazy and ignorant. Take the time to do it right.

Any letter you send to a school should emphasize that you want to attend that school and play for that specific team. Approach this process as you would a job interview.

You may suggest that you're looking for the best fit and best job, but you want to assure admissions officers and coaches that you are committed to and interested in attending their school. Universities want students who are focused and dedicated to their school, not someone who is simply shopping around. Market your academic strengths and mention why you're interested in their school. Never display your weaknesses. **Make sure that someone proofreads your letter for spelling and grammar.**

Your name
Address
City state zip
Phone
Email

Date

Dear Admissions Office,

I am interested in attending [University or College name] and studying [possible degree plans]. I am currently a [junior/senior] attending [name of high school] in [city, state]. I have a [G.P.A./honors student/ member of student group/ interested in --]. I believe that my [special skill, outstanding characteristic, community service, student involvement, summer jobs] makes me an asset for your school. [Now add a line about why you like that school - it has your major, you've watched their team for years, you've always dreamed of going there, etc]. Please send me information about your school's admission policies, financial aid, and athletics program.

Sincerely,

[Your name - sign it by hand legibly.]

Read the information you receive. You will begin to receive catalogs and brochures from all of these schools. You'll be flooded with information and mailings from some of them. If they tell you an admissions recruiter or school representative will travel through your area, attend. You'll gain valuable information about college even if you do not decide to attend that school. Also, return the questionnaires they send you and keep in contact if the school continues to look promising. You may be personally called by a representative. Do not be afraid to ask that person any questions you think of, and let your parents listen in and ask questions, too.

First say to yourself what you would be, and then do what you have to do.

- Epictetus

CHAPTER 4
STAND OUT STUDENTS

One of the best ways to market yourself as a strong candidate for an athletic scholarship is to be a good student. Good grades and good attendance make you a good prospect for several reasons. One, the coach won't have to worry about your academic eligibility. Two, the coach may be able to offer you a scholarship package that includes academic aid, allowing the program to save athletic funds for other needs. Finally, your good grades will assure the coach that you'll qualify for admission as well as be able to keep up your grades and studies under the pressure of traveling and playing during season.

Quality is not an act. It is a habit.
- Aristotle

Coaches understand that good students show up, do their work, and are responsible for their studies and grades. These good habits and characteristics often carry over to athletics. They help assure coaches that you'll get your work done and do your job in the game.

How do you get good grades? Whether you've always struggled in school or been a star student, there are ways you can improve.

- Go to class every day. Do not skip! Schedule doctor appointments or travel outside school hours so you can stay in class.

- Be on time and be prepared. Keep a planner and note the dates of quizzes and tests, write down your homework assignments, and watch for days when you have more than one test so you can study ahead of time.

- Do all your reading before class. Read the assigned chapters and study guides, and know what will be discussed before you go to class.

- Sit up front. Teachers will notice you and be more likely to write personal recommendations for your college and scholarship applications. Also, sitting in front forces you to focus and contribute in class.

> **WIN**
> **STAY ON TOP OF YOUR CLASSES**
> Keep track of your homework, quizzes, tests, and grades with a school planner.

- Turn in all your work on time.

- When you get your grades, ask to meet with the teacher to learn the correct answers and see how to improve.

- Participate in class. Answer the teacher's questions, talk to other students about the class topics, and take good notes to help your studies.

- If you're still struggling in class, ask a teacher to tutor you, or ask your parents to hire a tutor. Learning good study habits and techniques now will help you later!

> **TIME OUT!**
> **MAKING A PLAN**
>
> How do you find time to plan? Use what works for you, whether it's email, a web calendar, your cell phone, a journal, or post-it notes stuck to the fridge. But be sure to keep all your important dates and deadlines in one spot and update them regularly. Prioritize the most important tasks and do them first!

By failing to prepare, you are preparing to fail.
- Benjamin Franklin

Also make sure that you are completing your "core" classes for college prep, including the requisite hours of math, English, science, and other courses.

> **LOSS**
> **THINKING A 'C' AVERAGE WON'T AFFECT YOUR CHANCES**
> Get tutoring, schedule more time for studying, or talk to your teachers about extra credit. The stronger your grades, the better your chances.

CHAPTER 5
MOST VALUABLE
PLAYERS

How do you become one of the athletes who stands out on the field? It takes more than talent. It takes hard work and dedication. The star athlete will constantly look inward for ways to improve.

> **WIN**
> **TAKE LESSONS**
> Find a coach who can help you improve your weaknesses and get an edge on your game.

- To be a star athlete, start with yourself. Make a list of your strengths and weaknesses. Ask your parents, teammates, and coaches what you are good at and where you need to improve. Keep a list of these strengths to help market yourself. Take the list of weaknesses and start to improve in those areas through extra practice or special lessons.

- Be an "I'll fix it" athlete. Never make excuses. Coaches don't want to hear them. They want athletes with initiative. Find out what you did wrong and fix it. Ask for another chance to make it right and then make it right. Take another cut, another shot, another ball, and make yourself better. Never settle by giving up or ending on a bad play.

- Practice how you play. Every practice should be focused and committed. You should give 110% at practice. If you practice in a sloppy manner, recruiters won't take a second look. They want someone who works when people aren't looking, who takes extra time to practice, who works on fundamentals until they are perfect. No job is too small.

- Stay mentally focused in practice and in the game. It's just as important to train your mind as it is to train your muscles. Visualize the play. Work through it in your head. Stay in the moment mentally, and it will strengthen your game overall.

- Be a team player. That means show up early, help with equipment, be ready to play. If you're on the bench, cheer your teammates on. Don't point fingers or be negative. Be the leader in team spirit and encouragement.

Success is dependent upon effort.
- Sophocles

- Be ready and willing to do what it takes for your team to win. This may not always be playing your primary position or performing what you think is the best play for the game, but it's your job to play for your coach and the team.

Start by doing what is necessary, then what's possible and suddenly you are doing the impossible.
                    - St. Francis of Assisi

-   Be competitive but maintain good sportsmanship. This means playing with pride and a positive attitude. Never swear, throw things, or fight with a referee or another player. Keep your composure in the game and after the game.

-   Join a travel team if possible. Playing on year-round teams that travel and compete offers you more, and stronger, experience.

-   Attend sports camps for both skills and exposure. Skills camps will focus on improving your game, while exposure or college camps will invite coaches to watch you participate in group skill sets and practices.

RIDING THE BENCH

Even if you aren't in the game, you're still a part of the team. Taking your turn on the bench offers you a chance to rest, to watch the game, to learn from your coaches and teammates, and to show your dedication and support to the team. But it isn't always easy when you want to be out there playing. Here's how to survive and put your best foot forward.

- Cheer for your teammates. Wish them the best. You can want badly to play and still support those who are in the game.
- If you aren't sure why you aren't playing, try to catch the coach at practice (don't ambush him or her right after the game with your parents in tow) and ask how you can improve and get more playing time.
- If necessary, seek out lessons to improve your game.
- Ask your teammates for help. If one of your friends is great at lay-ups or hitting curveballs, ask them to show you how they do it.
- Increase your physical training to get in better shape.
- Be open to playing other positions. You may find a talent you didn't know you had!

Accomplishing all of this may seem challenging or impossible. Everyone has bad days.

Great works are performed not by strength, but by perseverance.
- Samuel Johnson

But, if you train your mind and spirit as well as your body, you will be able to handle tough losses and hard days with composure and dignity, which always stand out.

LOSS
PLAYING THE BLAME GAME
Don't whine about your team or the coach. Find things that you can fix in your own game instead.

39

CHAPTER 6
SCORING A
SCHOLARSHIP

A star candidate for an athletic scholarship will be both a star student and a star athlete. But there's more. They will be a standout! How do you stand out from the crowd? By working hard in the classroom and at practice, you'll get teachers and coaches buzzing about you. But there are other things you can do.

- Make yourself a well-rounded person. This means challenging yourself in areas where you may not feel comfortable or with things you don't often spend time doing. It may be student council or leadership for one student, scouting for another. You may join the debate team or try band. Maybe you spend a semester traveling or in FFA. Whatever it is, make time to try something new and outside your normal social circle. It will help you meet others, make connections, and gain valuable experience at what it will be like joining a new team in a new environment. Also, it will show you are a well-rounded person.

- Participate in your community. This may be through a church group, a school group, or on your own. You may help clean up a beach or sing carols at a nursing home at Christmas. Whatever it is, make a point to give time to your community and serve others. You may even help the youth in your community with a sports camp!

> **WIN**
> **VOLUNTEER**
> Try new things! Find something that you enjoy doing. Start by giving an hour or two and build up. Ask around your neighborhood and find out what's missing. Besides, giving back feels good!

A man wrapped up in himself makes a very small bundle.

- Ben Franklin

- Nurture relationships with your friends and family. These are the people who will support you and love you in the coming years. High school and college are challenging, and you'll need a strong, supportive safety net.

- Make sure that your parents are positive and encouraging toward your coach, team, and teammates. Their attitude makes a big difference. They should ask what they can do to help the team, not act as if the team owes something to their child. This is true even if you are paying to be on a travel team. Recruiters and coaches want to deal with agreeable parents, not troublemakers. Make sure they have made a good name for themselves—and you as well.

LOSS
EXPECTING THE COACH
TO FIND YOU
Don't wait for the coach
to ring your doorbell.
Market yourself.
Contact him or her and
make your pitch!

CHAPTER 7
PLAYING THE FIELD

Once you have narrowed your list of selected schools and know what you're looking for, you can begin to contact coaches to see who is interested in you. Although you may have begun with thirty or forty schools, after you read the information they have sent, you should have narrowed the list to fifteen or twenty.

Then, over the next year you can narrow this list, visit some schools, and end up with a solid list of six to twelve schools you're serious about.

43

Contact coaches in your junior year and let them know who you are, where you play, and why you want to play for them. This is your first impression, and it's important for you to be confident and professional. Provide the coach with information about you, how to contact you, and how or where to see you play.

If it is to be, it is up to me.
- Anon

WIN
HAVE MATERIALS READY
TO SEND TO COACHES
Keep copies and files of all your important athletic documents, such as your stats and Clearinghouse registration

---

On the next page is a sample coach's letter. Remember to highlight your achievements and your strengths. Again, make sure that someone proofreads your letter and checks your grammar.

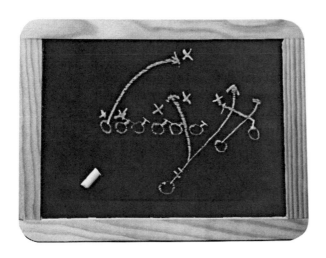

Your name
Address
City state zip
Phone
Email

Date

Dear Coach [fill in their name here],

I am interested in attending [University or College name] and playing [sport] as a [team name/mascot]. I am currently a [junior/senior] attending [name of high school] in [city, state]. I have been a [position] for [how many] years, and I also have experience at [other positions]. In addition, I have played for [enter any travel or elite teams here] for [how many] years.

I believe that my [special skill, outstanding characteristic] makes me an asset for your team. [You can also add statistics, G.P.A., community service or student involvement, summer jobs, or other commitments in another sentence]. [Now add a line about why you like that school— they have your major, you've watched them for years, you've always dreamed of going there, etc].

If you would like more information, I can send you my team booklet, statistics, a recruiting video, or any other information you may need. I have included the remaining dates of our tournament schedule for the summer in case you have the opportunity to see me play. I am excited about the possibility of playing for your team, and I hope to speak with you in the future.

Sincerely,
[Your name—sign it by hand, legibly.]

You may also want to attach documents to your letter, such as a current schedule for your high school or travel team, or your team's media guide. Do not attach more than one or two documents. It's best to save your current stats, newspaper clippings, and videos until coaches request them

If you are playing near your target school during the next year, you can send a short, polite email a week or so ahead of time to inform the recruiters of your games.

What if you or your team doesn't have a media guide? With a little help from coaches or parents, you can design your own. Let's take a look at what you need.

Media Guide/Booklet Contents

- team picture
- team name with coaches' names and contact
- info
- team roster listing name, #, position, and year
- list of tournament dates
- player profiles with individual pictures
  if available, including
    o Basic info such as #, position, year, etc.
    o major stats
    o personal interests
    o schools or majors student is interested in

This allows college coaches to contact your coach and arrange to watch you play in a tournament. Media guides are as varied as the teams they represent. You may staple some black and white copies together or take color pages into a copying service and have them bound. It all depends on the time, effort, and money you're willing to put forth. However, even the simplest booklet can look professional and convey the necessary information.

What about a video? These also needn't be complicated; you don't need a professional to have a strong video to submit. Find a cameraman with a steady hand and follow these tips.

Making a Video
- Introduce yourself. Smile. Wear a uniform shirt if possible so coaches can see your colors and number and identify you if they attend a tournament.
- Make two or three consecutive plays in each position you play. Illustrate both offensive and defensive skills. You may stop in between different skill sets and positions, but try to keep the camera rolling when making two or three plays in a row. Tapes can be edited, and coaches would rather see that you can make the same play twice. Of course, if you have a bad couple of plays, stop, rewind, and try again. You may also highlight any special skills, such as speed.
- Keep it short. A coach should be able to view the entire video in about five minutes.

Finally, keep yearly and current statistics for both high school and summer teams. You may send a prospective coach your team stats, highlighting your own abilities, or you may type up a page showing your stats only.

LOSS
EXPECTING YOUR HIGH SCHOOL COACH OR TRAVEL COACH TO DROP EVERYTHING TO MARKET YOU
If you need help with a media guide or a video, try to schedule a time when other juniors and seniors can participate. That way, you can help one another run through the drills.

CHAPTER 8
THE BUSINESS OF
SPORTS

Whether you realize it
or not, when you pursue
an athletic scholarship,
you are participating in
a business transaction.

You are networking,
assuring others of your competence, and signing a
contract for money and goods to be exchanged. To
be successful, you must master good manners and
the basics of professionalism.

Your number one concern should be how you
interact with others. Do more than treat others
as you would expect to be treated. Treat them as
you would expect the person you love and respect
most to be treated, whether it is your mother,
your grandmother, or someone else entirely. Do
more than is required, and your efforts will be
fondly remembered and returned.

Address adults as Mr. or Ms. until you are given
permission to do otherwise. Do this in your
letters, your phone calls, and your personal
meetings.

You may address coaches as Coach [last name] but do not use first names unless you are told to do so. Even then, you will want to speak with the utmost respect. Just because someone tells you to address them by a first name does not put you on the same level as them. Do not address or talk to coaches or recruiters as if they are your friends. You must continue to show respect in your speech and actions.

All doors open to courtesy.
- Thomas Fuller

If you do not know someone's name, use ma'am or sir when you speak. This does not occur nearly enough in today's world, and it will make you stand out as a person with good manners.

When you meet someone, look him or her in the eye, give a firm handshake, stand with your hands at your sides (not across your chest), and do not fidget. Your body language reveals a lot, and first impressions count!

Try to send letters instead of emails to make first contact with a coach. Again, you will stand out as someone who has taken extra time and care. Always thank the person for his or her time, whether you speak to a secretary or the coach. Never treat anyone badly or take their time and effort for granted; good news and bad news travels fast in athletic departments, and if you snub a secretary, the coach will hear about it, guaranteed.

Follow up visits or calls with real thank you letters. They don't need to be long. A simple note will do. Below is a sample.

> Dear Coach [last name],
> I enjoyed visiting the campus last weekend and meeting with you. I learned a great deal about the athletic program and the team, and I am excited about the prospect of playing for you. Thank you for your time. I look forward to speaking with you again.

Promptly return phone calls, emails, and letters. You should reply to any correspondence within three days. Phone calls and emails should be returned within a day or two.

If you take longer than a week to respond, you should have a good reason (you've been out of town or had a family emergency), and you should apologize and attempt to make yourself available at that person's convenience to speak again.

If you speak with someone on the phone or in person, give that person your full attention. Your cell phone should be off. Whatever you do, don't text or call or answer while you are with a coach or a recruiter. Try not to be distracted. Respond by asking thoughtful questions (which you may want to prepare ahead of time if you are nervous) and sharing a little about yourself.

Dress nicely when you are meeting someone. Wear business casual or church attire. This can be anything from a casual suit and tie or slacks and a button down for boys, and a dress, skirt, or slacks and a blouse for girls. You should never dress in athletic gear or sloppy attire.

Avoid wearing jeans unless you are attending a game or some other team event. Even then, pair them with a nice shirt or a polo. Wear nice shoes.

You should present yourself as someone who takes care of themselves and their appearance. You won't impress anyone if you show up with tangled hair, a T-shirt, and flip-flops. Remember, you're trying to earn a scholarship worth thousands of dollars. Look the part.

Always be polite. Good manners go beyond please and thank you, sir or ma'am. Use proper table manners if you go to dinner. Demonstrate simple courtesies, such as holding the door open for the person behind you. Be on your best behavior.

> **WIN**
> **PUT YOUR BEST FOOT FORWARD**
> The first time you meet someone will always leave an impression. Make sure it's a good one.

Be positive rather than negative. This is important to you as a team player and as a person. Look at the bright side. Offer your opinions if asked, but do not complain or criticize.

If you're on a team visit where you spend time with other players, do not participate in anything illegal. This is a time for you to have fun and enjoy the school, but not a time to be thrown off campus for underage drinking or drug experimentation. A player may be thrown off a team for that type of behavior; you'll simply be banished from the school

with no chance for admission or scholarship.

LOSS
CUTTING LOOSE ON SCHOOL VISITS
Just because you're away from home doesn't mean you can act irresponsibly without consequences.

Finally, try to remember the golden rule—treat others as you would want your grandmother treated. Use your best manners in person or on the phone. Dress nicely. Return calls quickly. Be polite. Be yourself at your best.

Use these tips and you will stand out from the crowd as an exceptional athlete worthy of attending school under scholarship.

CHAPTER 9
COMPLETING THE
REQUIREMENTS

You'll need to get your transcripts and records in order to apply for scholarships and to be eligible for recruiting. One requirement that you will have to fulfill is to achieve a minimum score on the SAT or ACT. Schools have different minimum requirements, and the required score may also be altered by your grades and the strength of the rest of your application.

Testing

You will need to take the SAT and probably the ACT in your junior year. Most schools accept both; some accept only one or the other. However, taking both will help in marketing yourself because schools will be able to use the higher number for your admissions application.

**WIN
PRACTICE FOR THE
TEST**
Find practice tests in books, on discs, or online. Run several simulations where you sit for two or three hours, time yourself, and focus on areas to improve.

The SAT is broken into verbal, mathematics, analytical, and essay.

Your section scores will be added together with your essay to compute your SAT score for admission applications.

You can take the SAT and ACT more than once to raise your score. When you take the SAT more than once, most schools will take your overall highest score.

For instance, you can add your highest verbal with your highest math; the two scores do not need to be from the same testing date. Give yourself a couple months between tests to rest, study, and review to improve your score.

**LOSS
WAITING UNTIL THE
LAST TESTING DAY**
Make sure you leave yourself time to retest to get the best scores possible.

TESTING PREP

SAT website and registration
www.Collegeboard.com

ACT website and registration
www.Actstudent.org

Testing tips
www.Powerprep.com

Tutoring centers
www.reportcard.sylvan.info
www.kaptest.com

TESTING TIPS

- Study three to six months before the test. Go online or buy books with practice tests. Take one or two of these under time and pressure similar to the real test day. Then go back and review your correct and incorrect answers. Use this as a study guide for your weaknesses, and focus on those areas prior to the test.
- Get help. Take a class or go to a tutor to learn valuable testing tricks. You can learn when it helps your score to guess and when it hurts, how to judge the best answers, evaluate when the test is getting more difficult, when to skip ahead for time, and how to make educated guesses.
- A few days before the test, take another practice test. Review your incorrect answers and take the last few days to memorize formulas or vocabulary that gives you trouble.
- The night before, eat a good meal and get a good night's sleep.
- On test day get up at least an hour before to allow yourself time to wake up. Take a pencil, pen, paper, and a calculator with you, depending upon testing regulations. Eat a good breakfast and get there in time to provide your ID and check in.

Then try to relax; you've prepared, and you can always take it again.

Clearinghouse

If you are interested in any NCAA schools, or
those coaches are interested in you, you will need
to apply to the NCAA Clearinghouse. The
Clearinghouse is one-stop shopping for NCAA
athletic coaches. The Clearinghouse makes sure
you are eligible for recruitment and warehouses all
your transcript, grade, and testing information. It
is your responsibility to provide them with this
data by instructing your high school and testing
center to send them the information. Go online to
the Clearinghouse site NCAAclearinghouse.net and
fill out the forms. In order to provide complete
transcripts and testing information, you have to
wait until the end of your junior year, but your
profile must be complete before you sign and
accept a scholarship with an NCAA school.

Recruiting Rules

The NCAA and NAIA have different recruiting
regulations. Further, NCAA has more stringent
recruiting regulations for Division I Athletics than
for Divisions II and III. Each sport has its own
recruiting windows and contact/dead periods. See
the respective websites for your sport-specific
dates.

CHAPTER 10
FIRST TALKS TO
COLLEGE VISITS

Once you have spoken with, or been contacted by, a college coach or recruiter, the real recruiting process has begun. If they're talking to you, they're interested.

Now it is their responsibility, and yours, to discover whether you're right for that team. The coach may ask you for more information on your grades and statistics, or come to watch you play.

I'm a great believer in luck, and I find the harder I work, the more I have of it.

- Thomas Jefferson

By now you should have an idea of what you are looking for in a school and athletic program, and be able to determine whether you like what you see.

These conversations are an opportunity for you to make sure you understand the team and the school and that they fit what you are looking for. You can do this through phone calls and meetings, but the best way to evaluate a school is to visit it.

COACH'S CORNER

WHAT COACHES WANT
By Christina Weiser
Assistant Softball Coach, Regis University

Players who take advantage of their opportunities and **work for what they want.**

Players who are **proactive.** Don't wait for us to contact you; send us a letter and a video, and let us know where you'll be playing.

Players who **hustle** on and off the field—never walk.

Players who take **pride** in their appearance. Keep your uniform tucked in—it shows you pay attention to the little things.

Players with **self-control.** Act responsibly and control your attitude. NEVER throw equipment or lose your temper.

Once you've narrowed your list of schools to five to ten, it's time to start visiting. You may visit on your own, or you may go as part of a recruiting trip when the coach and players show you around, answer questions, and put their best foot forward. Under NCAA regulations, a player can only receive five official visits paid for by the schools. However, you can still visit schools on your own dime. If you've come this far, you've done well, but some important decisions still lie ahead.

If any of these schools have offered you a campus visit, tour weekend, or a place to stay, grab it! The cost of this trip may come out of your own pocket or it may be paid for by the athletic department, but you'll probably at least get some free cafeteria meals, a tour of campus, and a look at the surrounding community.

These trips are the best way to choose a college. If you go during the school year, you may be able to get an absence waiver from your high school. Then, you'll have the opportunity to stay with some students, talk with them openly, and ask anything you didn't want to ask the admissions counselor.

WIN
TAKE NOTES
During your visit, take notes on the best classes and teachers, places to eat, and things you should know. That way, when you get to campus as a freshman, you'll have a leg up on everyone.

Ask to be introduced to students enrolled in your desired major and involved in the activities that interest you, and request in advance to attend some classes. (If you're visiting one of your top two or three schools, find out a few of the best teachers in your major and write down their names; it will come in handy when you try to register for classes.)

Use your college visits as a way to ask questions and get a feel for each place. You should make every effort to talk to everyone you see: professors, players, students, coaches, and staff. By talking to different people on campus, you will get a full impression of both the college atmosphere and the environment where you'll spend the next four years. Also, try to sit in on a class for your major. It will give you an idea of what to expect your freshman year.

Don't forget to tour dorms, cafeterias, gyms, classrooms, computer labs, the recreation center, and the student center.

Sample Questions to Ask Students and Teachers

- What is the best feature of this college?
- What sets this school apart?
- What has been your experience here?
- What is a typical day for a student?
- What is the typical class size?
- Who will teach me? Teaching assistants or full professors?
- What degree plans are offered in my major?

Make sure to catch a game, or at least watch a practice. Meet some of the team. Get a feel for the school and the team. Imagine yourself as part of it.

Then ask yourself, does this feel right for me?

LOSS
NEGATIVITY

Coaches or students may be interested in which schools are recruiting you or where else you have visited. Be careful in your responses. You want the college you're visiting to know you're interested, but if you speak too negatively of the other coaches or schools, your guide may be wary of what you will say about them.

Questions to Ask the Coach or Team

- How would you describe the athletic program? The team? The coach's style?
- What is a typical day for a student athlete?
- What does a typical practice/season consist of?
- What are the expectations of the students? Players?
- What percentage of athletes graduate in four years?
- What type of scholarships are offered and what are the requirements?
- Will I be expected or allowed to take summer school?
- What type of aid will be available for summer courses?
- What happens if I get injured?
- Where do you see me playing?
- How many credits does the typical player take in season and out of season?
- How long does it take most of the student athletes to graduate?
- What is the team GPA?
- How long has the coach been at this school and does he or she have an extended contract?
- What other means of financial aid are available?
- Will I be able to have other employment?
- Are there restrictions on my extracurricular activities?
- What type of academic support is available?

CHAPTER 11 ~ CLUTCH TIME

How do you choose?

By now you should have a small list of potential schools that interest you.

Write these schools down and list five to ten pros and cons for each. Then attempt to narrow these schools to a list of your top five and rank them by the factors most important to you.

WIN
APPLY TO SEVERAL SCHOOLS

Apply to at least four different schools at different levels of play. This will give you options, as well as a safety net if things don't work out like you hope.

If you're talented and fortunate enough to be offered several scholarships, you'll have the benefit of choosing the best package for you.

Many students will find that the school they've been working with most closely, or had the most communication with, is the school they'll be drawn to. Others will have a lifelong affiliation with another, and there will be no question where they want to spend their next four years.

When applying to schools, you should send out five to ten applications to your dream, realistic, and safety schools. This will ensure that you have somewhere to go to school, even if the scholarships do not come from where you expect them. Ask coaches and schools whether application fee waivers are available.

Applications
Watch the deadlines! Coaches recruiting you will be aware of them, but they will also be busy with their own commitments.

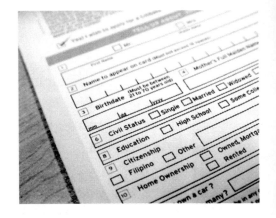

No one can apply and do the work but you!
Be responsible and prepared. Make a list of your top schools and the deadlines for admissions and financial aid. Stick to them faithfully. These schools do not have admissions policies for procrastinators. Make sure that you have copies of your transcript and extracurricular activities handy. Know your current GPA. Ask two or three of your favorite teachers, coaches, or principals if they will write a recommendation for you.

Give your references at least two to three weeks notice before your recommendation has to be ready. Take some time to sit with them and talk about your activities, or give them a list of your accomplishments. Even if they know how excellent you are in the classroom, they may not be aware of your achievements in other areas, or of your other time commitments after school. Tell them anything pertinent.

LOSS
IGNORING
DEADLINES
Make sure you get everything ready a few weeks ahead. You never know when you might need extra time to include something additional.

Apply carefully.
Type your application on a typewriter or a computer and then **Proofread your application**! Have others read over your application (which should be completed as neatly as possible) and look for errors and misspellings.

Do not rely on spellcheck!

Ask your high school English teacher or your counselor for help with your essay. Remember to be honest, but always represent yourself in your best light. Focus on and accentuate your strengths. Include anything that sets you apart and highlights your talents.

COACH'S CORNER

TIPS FOR A WINNING APPLICATION ESSAY

By Sue Beebe, Director first-year English,
Texas State University-San Marcos

Tell a story only you can tell. This needn't be dramatic or sensational, but it should be interesting. Think of something you have experienced and draw an interesting or unique conclusion from it.

Reflect. **Your essay should illustrate a level of reflection and understanding that shows you are prepared and ready for college.** Use your voice.

Reveal a sense of yourself. The way you choose detail and write your essay should reveal who you are. **Let the judges get to know you.**

Connect with your reader. Your reader should understand and be moved by your essay. **Ultimately your essay will reveal your personality as well as your skills.**

Financial aid

Do not neglect other types of aid. There are scholarships for many things besides athletics, including hobbies and other extracurriculars, academics, local charitable associations, and various groups.

Many things are lost for want of asking.

- English Proverb

Ask your guidance counselor for a list of local scholarships, look on the web for scholarships in areas where you excel, and apply for everything you find. If you cover some of your aid this way, it will make you an even more attractive candidate for your favored athletic team.

You (and often your parents) must fill out a **Free Application for Federal Student Aid (FAFSA) which is needed for most types of financial aid, grants, work study, loans, and scholarships.**

You may delay, but time will not.
- Ben Franklin

This application is available in the financial aid office, high school counselor's office, public libraries, and online at **www.fafsa.ed.gov.** Your FAFSA should be completed as soon as possible after January of your senior year. It often relies on income tax figures, so make sure your parents are on top of early tax filing. You may also use last year's figures, submit the form, and update the information as soon as possible. This will make you eligible for scholarships as well as other types of financial aid. You may also reference www.finaid.org or www.fastweb.com for more financial aid and scholarship information.

COACH'S CORNER

THE INS AND OUTS OF FINANCIAL AID

By Dora Sims, Director of Financial Aid
Alvin Community College

Deadline dates vary by schools. University deadlines may be as early as February 28, and community colleges or open-door schools as late as June 30. **The importance of the deadline date is that most funds are limited; therefore, they are awarded on a first come, first served basis.**

Students should apply for grants and federal aid with a FAFSA. Many students feel that they will not qualify based on income. However, all income ranges qualify for some type of assistance. **Always apply. The worst that can happen is that you don't receive aid.**

Apply for every scholarship you qualify for. I can't tell you how many times I make students apply and **they get the scholarship because they are the only applicants. Apply for everything.**

In applying for scholarships, applicants should **make a copy of that application and complete it in pencil first,** have someone else review it for spelling and grammar, and then follow the instructions (print or type as indicated, use black ink only, and include a self-stamped, self-addressed envelope).

CHAPTER 12 ~ PUTTING IT ON PAPER

The CONTRACT

Congratulations! A coach wants you to play for his/her team. Now what?

Allow the coach to mention the contract and make an offer. You may show interest, but don't be over-eager. It helps to say that you're still considering one or two other schools so the coach doesn't think that he/she can get you too easily or cheaply.

Listen to the offer. Consult with your parents. Some negotiation will probably be allowed, even expected. You may ask if that's the best offer the program is able to make and wait to see whether you get a better one. Or tell them that you really want to come and play, but you're worried about the cost of books, additional loans, or anything else that they may be able to add to your offer.

Once you accept, the coach will ask you to sign a contract.

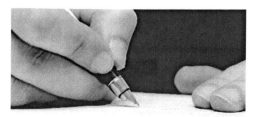

When a coach recruits you, makes you an offer, and you accept, you will sign a letter of intent, which is essentially a contract stating you will play for that team. The letter of intent guarantees that you are eligible, will attend, and will participate in the athletics program in exchange for athletic or financial aid for one year.

These contracts are written for one year, but may be renewable for up to four years. Once you sign this, you may not change your mind without penalty.

WIN
NEGOTIATE FOR THE MOST MONEY
Use your strengths and try for the best deal possible.

LOSS
TELLING THE COACH WHAT YOU'RE WORTH
Don't overstep your bounds. Let the coach lead the way.

For more information, log on to www.national-letter.org

BUT WHAT ABOUT?

CONTACT AND DEAD PERIODS?

Contact periods and dead periods in recruiting do not prohibit you from speaking with the admissions office or other academic departments at your target schools. You just can't have contact with the coach or a team rep. Each NCAA division or sport has different contact periods from the junior year into the senior year.

Check the NCAA website for details on your sport at www.ncaa.org

EARLY DECISION?

Early decision means you've chosen the school you want to attend in the fall and are committed to attending that school only. If you accept an early decision admission or scholarship, you should not apply to any other schools. If you are offered a good scholarship from a school that you love, this may be a good way to ensure your spot on the team. This does not stop you from applying for other outside financial aid or individual scholarships.

WALK-ONS?

So, what if the coach can't offer you a scholarship, but you know that it's the school and program for you? You can always "walk-on," or try out in the fall of your freshman year. Different schools handle walk-on players differently; there may be an established tryout period, or you may practice with the team for a week or so. If you are interested in this option, contact the coach and ask permission to walk on. Then, find out what you will need to do to try out for the team.

TRANSFERS?

So, maybe you want to stay close to home for another year or two, strengthen your G.P.A., save some money, or develop your skills. Attending a junior college and transferring later may be the option for you. After two years of junior college, you will have basic core classes out of the way, as well as have valuable experience in college athletics. Further, you may receive a lot more playing time while in junior college and become a stronger candidate for a scholarship. As an added bonus, you'll probably have a much better idea of which program or school really interests you after getting a feel for collegiate play. A few tips: Be sure to take only core classes so all your credits will transfer! Electives may not carry over. Also, if you're struggling in classes, don't be afraid to sign up for the "intro" sections. They may not transfer for credit but they will prepare you for success in college courses.

CHAPTER 13 ~ WHAT TO EXPECT FROM YOUR FRESHMAN YEAR

When it comes time to leave home and head off to college to begin your life as a student athlete, you'll be one of the few talented and fortunate players to have the experience of playing collegiate sports. Whether you've chosen a Division I school or a junior college to begin your journey, you'll be attending college as a student athlete.

You'll have many things to juggle as a student athlete: being a college freshman, finding and attending your classes, living away from home, attending practice and playing for a new team, passing your classes, and working towards graduation. You will have to fit in time for classes, practice, studying, eating, sleeping, laundry, training and conditioning, roommates, social commitments, etc. Also, remember that college is often a chance for people to discover more about themselves. You may reinvent yourself, rethink issues that you took for granted, or find new interests at school. That's all part of the journey.

COACH'S CORNER

STANDOUT COLLEGE STUDENTS
By Laura Sauceda, Ph.D. Candidate
University of Texas - Austin

Students who stand out are engaged in the classroom, demonstrate genuine effort such as asking questions, responding to other students during discussions, and seeking help during office hours.

Students have to learn how to balance and budget their time. They have to make sure they have their priorities straight so that nothing slips through the cracks. **Cramming doesn't work. Neither does turning in subpar work.** Players can't play ball if they can't pass.

The **students who encounter problems have usually overwhelmed themselves and lost balance between school and their extracurricular activities.** When they lose their focus, they often don't know how they are doing in classes and may wait until too late to try to improve their grades.

Don't let it happen to you!

Expect to work hard at school and at practice. Stay healthy, make good choices, surround yourself with positive influences, and enjoy the college experience to the fullest. It will be a challenge but it will make you a strong person as well.

WIN
BE AN 'I'LL DO IT' PLAYER

Whether it's cleaning up after practice or a game, or putting in some extra practice, be a player who steps up and says, "I'll do it!"

LOSS
THINKING THE LAW DOESN'T APPLY

Just because you're at college doesn't mean you won't go to jail or be arrested for breaking the law for underage drinking or experimenting with drugs. Stay clean!

They conquer who believe they can.

- John Dryden

Finally, remember all the years you worked to achieve this, and enjoy it!

RESOURCES

College Finder and SAT site
www.CollegeBoard.com

National Collegiate Athletic Association
www.NCAA.org

NCAA rankings in all divisions
NCAAsports.com

National Association of Intercollegiate Athletics
www.NAIA.org

National Junior College Athletic Association
www.NJCAA.org

Clearinghouse – register and upload your info
NCAAclearinghouse.net

National Letter Intent Information
www.national-letter.org

ACT website
www.actstudent.org

FAFSA site
www.fafsa.ed.gov

Financial Aid Info
www.Finaid.org

Financial Aid Opportunities and Scholarships
www.fastweb.com

US News *college rankings*
www.Usnews.com/usnews/edu

Princeton Review and the cost of colleges
Princetonreview.com/college/

College and scholarship searches
Colleges.com

Scholarship giveaways, applying for aid, understanding award letters
Collegeanswer.com

Tutoring Sylvan and Kaplan
www.Reportcard.sylvan.info
www.Kaptest.com

SAT daily testing tips
powerprep.com

Insider information

Yahoo.com/education/higher_education/colleges_and_universities/

Don't forget to look at online meeting places like Myspace for student contacts. Check with school booster clubs for contacts and info, too.

RUMORS AT THE WATER COOLER

Have you heard the latest myths about college? Don't make these assumptions:

- **That you can take the summer off or stop your training before college.** College will make you train harder than ever before! Your body loses muscle mass after three days without exercise. Your skills and techniques can get rusty in a week or two. Stay on top of your game.

- **That college will be a breeze.** You'll have more schoolwork to do than ever before. It will take scheduling, hard work, and dedication. Don't fall behind.

- **That you will play the same position you try out for.** Once you play for a team, you may be moved to different areas, shifted back and forth to work with various players, or even be switched to another position. Be flexible.

- **That you should pick your school by your major.** A large percentage of students change their majors; some even change it several times. Schools can also drop the major you're in love with. Find a school that's strong in areas that interest you, but don't base your decision solely on the program in your intended major.

- **That playing for a particular team will make up for other areas of your life.** Find a school that feels right for you. Many students don't complete their play for various reasons. They may get burnt out, find a job or a mate that changes their priorities, or even suffer an injury. Find a place where you'll be happy, even if you aren't on the team.

IF I KNEW THEN WHAT I KNOW NOW...

WHAT REAL COLLEGE FRESHMAN WISH THEY HAD KNOWN

- The amount of work in high school drastically changes. In college it may take two to three days instead of two to three hours to prepare for a test.

- The average grade is a C. Even though you made A's in high school, you may be making C's now.

- You need to get to know your teachers. This lets you find out what the teachers expect as well as get help if you need it.

- There is a lot of free time, but it has to be budgeted for studying or the work will overwhelm you.

- Parking on campus is impossible. It may be easier to carpool or take the bus to get around.

EJECTIONS AND FOULS

What's guaranteed to make you miss out on your dream of getting a sports scholarship?

Don't:

- Act like a prima donna player who always needs accommodation.
- Think the team relies on you—confidence and cockiness are two different things.
- Place all your bets on one or two schools even if their coaches have talked to you. If your target schools haven't made you an offer, don't assume they will. This is how the courting process works.
- Shrug off admissions applications because a coach is talking to you.

COMPLETE LIST OF WINNERS

KEEP IMPORTANT DOCUMENTS ON FILE

IMAGINE YOUR IDEAL COLLEGE, TEAM, AND PLAYING SEASON

ATTEND A SKILLS CAMP

PICK A SCHOOL THAT FITS ALL YOUR NEEDS

THINK OF HOW YOUR EXPECTATIONS AND IDEALS MIGHT FIT INTO THESE CATEGORIES

STAY ON TOP OF YOUR CLASSES

TAKE LESSONS

VOLUNTEER

HAVE MATERIALS READY TO SEND TO COACHES

PRACTICE FOR THE TEST

PUT YOUR BEST FOOT FORWARD

TAKE NOTES

APPLY TO SEVERAL SCHOOLS

NEGOTIATE FOR THE MOST MONEY

BE AN 'I'LL DO IT' PLAYER

LOSSES TO AVOID

IGNORING OTHER TYPES OF AID

ASSUMING YOU WILL PLAY D-1

CHOOSING A SCHOOL OR A TEAM BECAUSE SOMEONE ELSE WANTS IT

PICKING A SCHOOL WITHOUT VISITING

SENDING OUT SLOPPY MAIL

THINKING A 'C' AVERAGE WON'T AFFECT YOUR CHANCES

PLAYING THE BLAME GAME

EXPECTING THE COACH TO FIND YOU

EXPECTING YOUR HIGH SCHOOL COACH OR TRAVEL COACH TO DROP EVERYTHING TO MARKET YOU

CUTTING LOOSE ON SCHOOL VISITS

WAITING UNTIL THE LAST TESTING DAY

NEGATIVITY

IGNORING DEADLINES

TELLING THE COACH WHAT YOU'RE WORTH

THINKING THE LAW DOESN'T APPLY

INSPIRATIONS

A journey of a thousand miles must begin with a single step.
- Chinese proverb

Do what you can, with what you have, where you are.
- Theodore Roosevelt

Always bear in mind that your own resolution to success is more important than any other one thing.
- Abraham Lincoln

First say to yourself what you would be, and then do what you have to do.
- Epictetus

Quality is not an act. It is a habit.
- Aristotle

By failing to prepare, you are preparing to fail.
- Benjamin Franklin

Success is dependent upon effort.
- Sophocles

Start by doing what is necessary, then what's possible and suddenly you are doing the impossible.
- St. Francis of Assisi

Great works are performed not by strength, but by perseverance.
- Samuel Johnson

A man wrapped up in himself makes a very small bundle.
- Ben Franklin

If it is to be, it is up to me.
- Anon

All doors open to courtesy.
- Thomas Fuller

I'm a great believer in luck, and I find the harder I work, the more I have of it.
- Thomas Jefferson

Many things are lost for want of asking.
- English Proverb

You may delay, but time will not.
- Ben Franklin

They conquer who believe they can.
- John Dryden

To purchase additional copies of <u>The Student Athlete Handbook for the 21st Century</u>, order online through Paypal at <u>studentathletehandbook21.com</u> or send this order form with a check to

CG Legacy Foundation
350 N Guadalupe St. Suite 140
PMB 420
San Marcos, TX 78666

Each copy is $14.95 + $3.50 S&H
(TX residents, please add 8.25% for tax)

An example for Texas residents: two copies would be
$14.95 x 1.0825 = $16.18 x 2=$32.36
Plus $3.50 x 2 = $7.00
Total amount would be $39.36

Please indicate the total number of copies needed here:_____

Where did you hear about the book?

_____

For bulk quantities, purchase inquiries, or information on seminars, please contact
CG Legacy Foundation at

<u>cg@studentathletehandbook21.com</u>
or
<u>studentathletehandbook21@hotmail.com</u>

ACKNOWLEDGEMENTS

I would like to thank all those who helped make this possible. Thanks to Tracy Staton, Sue Beebe, Dora Sims, Laura Sauceda, Philip Chalk, Jill Hays, Christina Weiser, Laura Ellis, and Edward Lai for your contributions, which helped make this project a success.

Also, I would like to thank my wonderful coaches who trained and taught me to be a successful student athlete, the teachers and professors who challenged me to a lifetime of learning, my parents and family for their unending support, and all my friends for their belief in my dreams.

And, thank you Brian, for your continued support, belief, and love.

About the author

Christine Grimes played competitive fastpitch softball for seventeen years, including 5A high school and elite travel ball, and went on to earn an out-of-state Division II athletic scholarship to Regis University. She graduated with honors in business and English and went on to complete two master's degrees in English. She has also coached at the high school and elite travel ball levels and has worked closely with coaches at the collegiate level.

CPSIA information can be obtained at www.ICGtesting.com
Printed in the USA
270145BV00003B/116/P